♭ **TENOR SAXOPHONE**  **LEVEL 1**

BELWIN 21st Century BAND METHOD
by JACK BULLOCK and ANTHONY MAIELLO

Congratulations on choosing to play a musical instrument. You will have many hours and many years of fun playing and performing in the band. This book has everything you need to learn to play. If you would like to know more, there is a video just for your instrument. You can play along at home with the CD accompaniments, with SmartMusic™ accompaniments or with the video—just as if you were in the band! You now belong to a special group of people around the world—people who love to make music, now and into the 21st Century!

WELCOME TO THE BAND!

from all of us at Alfred Publishing Co., Inc.,

Jack Bullock and Anthony Maiello

Editor: Thom Proctor
Production Coordinator: Edmond Randle
Cover Photo: Roberto Santos
Technical Editor: Dale Sloman
Finale Engraver: Rosario Ortiz
Art Design: Joseph Klucar
Art Coordinator: Thais Yanes

Saxophone on cover courtesy of THE SELMER COMPANY, INC.

PRACTICE MAKES BETTER:

Make time to practice every day. Pick a place where you will have good light and good air circulation, and where you will not be bothered. You should have plenty of room for a good chair and your music stand so you keep good position and posture. Keep track of how many minutes you practice. Work hard and have fun playing!

Week	Date	LESSON ASSIGNMENT	Sun.	Mon.	Tues.	Wed.	Thurs.	Fri.	Sat.	Total
1										
2										
3										
4										
5										
6										
7										
8										
9										
10										
11										
12										
13										
14										
15										
16										
17										
18										
19										
20										
21										
22										
23										
24										
25										
26										
27										
28										
29										
30										
31										
32										
33										
34										
35										
36										

Practice can be even better and more fun if you play along with the CD accompaniments, with SmartMusic™ accompaniments or with the video for your instrument. Ask your teacher or at your music store for more information on these products.

GET READY TO PLAY

STAFF

A Staff has five lines and four spaces.

CLEF SIGN

A clef sign is a symbol placed on the staff.

A B C D E F G A B C D E F G

The first seven letters of the alphabet
are used in music to name the lines and spaces.

Names of the Lines and Spaces.

BAR LINE AND MEASURE

bar lines

measure

A bar line is a line drawn through the staff.
A measure is the distance between two bar lines.

FINAL BAR LINE

A final bar line has a thin bar line
and a thick bar line which indicates the end.

TIME SIGNATURE

There are four counts in four/four time.

A time signature is placed at the beginning of the
staff and indicates the number of counts in a measure.

NOTE

Note heads   stem   flag

The parts of a note.

ACCIDENTALS

Flats, Sharps, and Naturals are called accidentals.

Whole Note

Receives four counts of sound in 4/4 time.

Whole Rest

Receives four counts of silence in 4/4 time.

Lesson 1

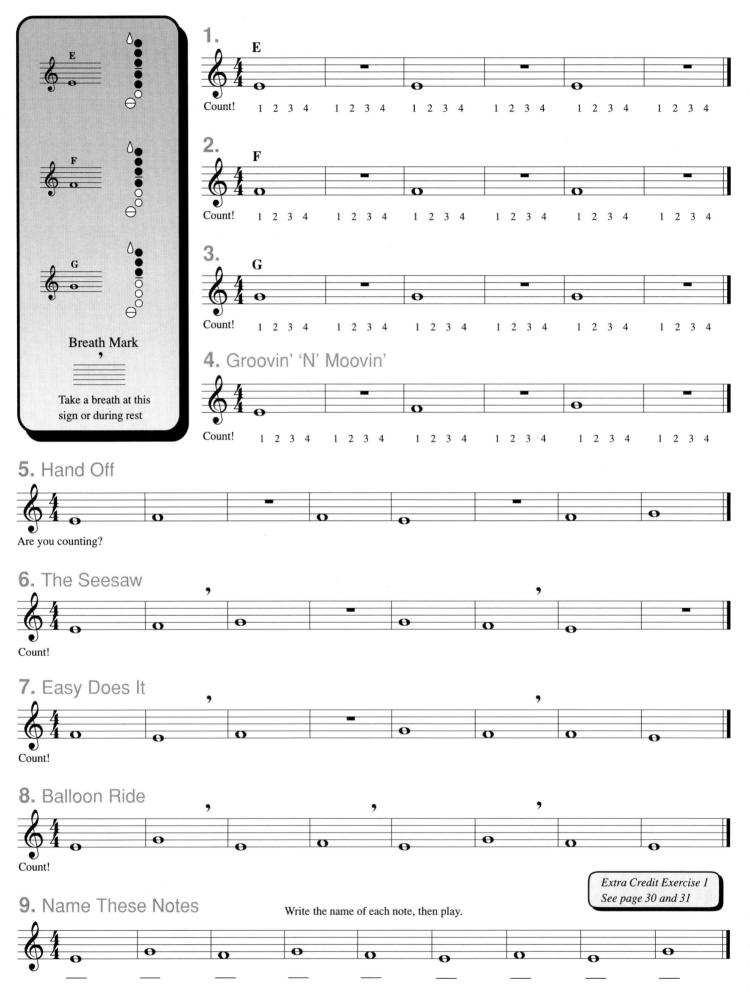

E

F

G

Breath Mark
'

Take a breath at this sign or during rest

1.

E

Count! 1 2 3 4   1 2 3 4   1 2 3 4   1 2 3 4   1 2 3 4   1 2 3 4

2.

F

Count! 1 2 3 4   1 2 3 4   1 2 3 4   1 2 3 4   1 2 3 4   1 2 3 4

3.

G

Count! 1 2 3 4   1 2 3 4   1 2 3 4   1 2 3 4   1 2 3 4   1 2 3 4

4. Groovin' 'N' Moovin'

Count! 1 2 3 4   1 2 3 4   1 2 3 4   1 2 3 4   1 2 3 4   1 2 3 4

5. Hand Off

Are you counting?

6. The Seesaw

Count!

7. Easy Does It

Count!

8. Balloon Ride

Count!

Extra Credit Exercise 1
See page 30 and 31

9. Name These Notes

Write the name of each note, then play.

Lesson 2

1.

D

Counting: 1 2 3 4   1 2 3 4   1 2 3 4   1 2 3 4   1 2 3 4   1 2 3 4

2.

C

Counting: 1 2 3 4   1 2 3 4   1 2 3 4   1 2 3 4   1 2 3 4   1 2 3 4

3. Half Note Trip

Counting: 1 2 3 4   1 2 3 4   1 2 3 4   1 2 3 4   1 2 3 4   1 2 3 4

4. Jive With Five

G   F   E

Counting: 1 2 3 4   1 2 3 4   1 2 3 4   1 2 3 4   1 2 3 4   1 2 3 4

5. Hot Cross Buns

Traditional, U.S.A.

Are you counting?

6. Dippin' Down

7. At Pierrot's Door

French Folk Song

8. Tune For Two
(Duet)*

Practice 8 and then 9. Then play 8 and 9 together as a duet.

9.

*Duet: A piece for two performers to play together.

5

Lesson 3

Quarter Note

Receives one count
in 4/4 time

Quarter Rest

Receives one count
in 4/4 time

Go To Next Line

Continue on next line
to final bar line without
stopping

1.

Counting: 1 2 3 4   1 2 3 4   1 2 3 4   1 2 3 4   1 2 3 4   1 2 3 4

2.

Counting: 1 2 3 4   1 2 3 4   1 2 3 4   1 2 3 4   1 2 3 4   1 2 3 4

3. Lightly Row   German Folk Song

(go to next line)

4. Lullaby   Kashmiri Folk Song

5. Dodo, L'Enfant Dors
(Sleep, Baby Sleep)   Belgian Folk Song

Extra Credit Exercise 2

6. Some Folks
(Duet)   Practice each separately, then play 6 and 7 as a duet.   Stephen Collins Foster, U.S.A.

7.

8. Draw a clef sign and a time signature. Then draw the bar lines. Write the counting beneath the line and then play.

6

Lesson 4

1.

2. New Note Rock

3. Rocket Ride

A

Repeat sign

Go back to the beginning and repeat

2/4 Time Signature

2 - two counts in each measure
4 - a quarter note receives one count

4. Scaling Up And Down

Don't take a breath until the first quarter rest.

5. Chorale
(Duet)

Practice 5 and 6 separately, then play as a duet.

6.

7. Tzena, Tzena, Tzena, Tzena (Rock)

Israeli Folk Song

8. Tenor Saxophone Workout

7

Extra Credit Exercise 3

Songs For The Fun Of It

Jingle Bells

James Pierpont, U.S.A.

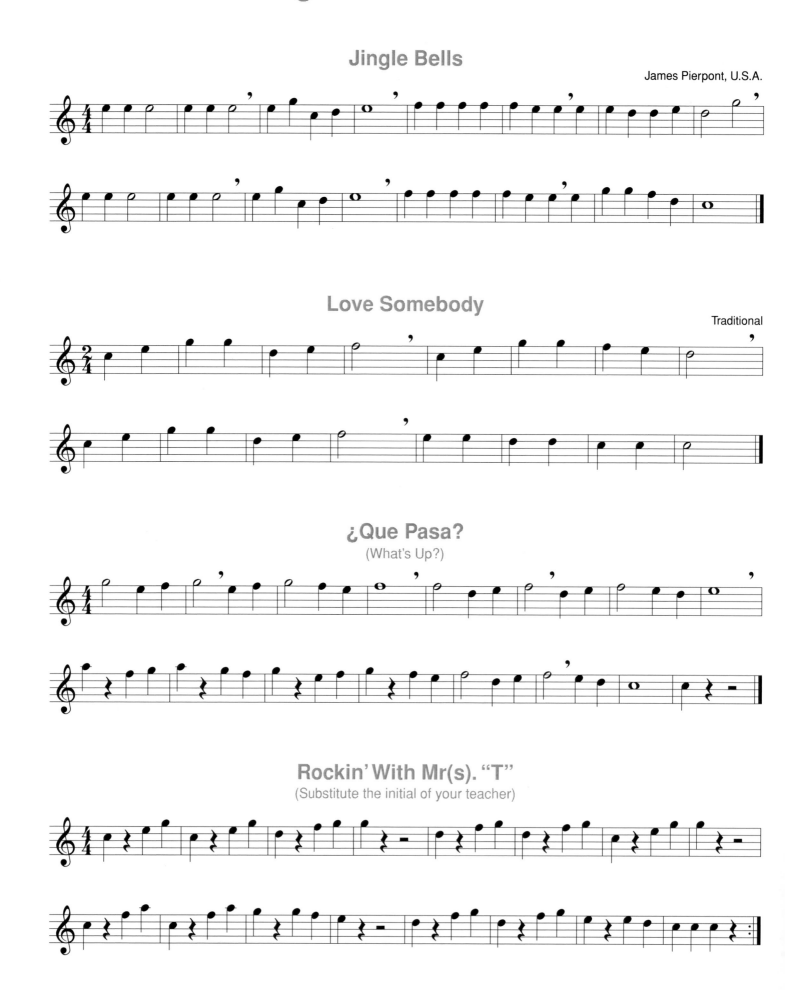

Love Somebody

Traditional

¿Que Pasa?
(What's Up?)

Rockin' With Mr(s). "T"
(Substitute the initial of your teacher)

Our First Concert

Alpha March

Jack Bullock, U.S.A.

Arroro Mi Niño

Argentine Folk Song

Jolly Old St. Nicholas

Traditional

The Saints Go Marching In

James M. Black and
Katherine E. Purvis, U.S.A.

Introduction

Lesson 5

10

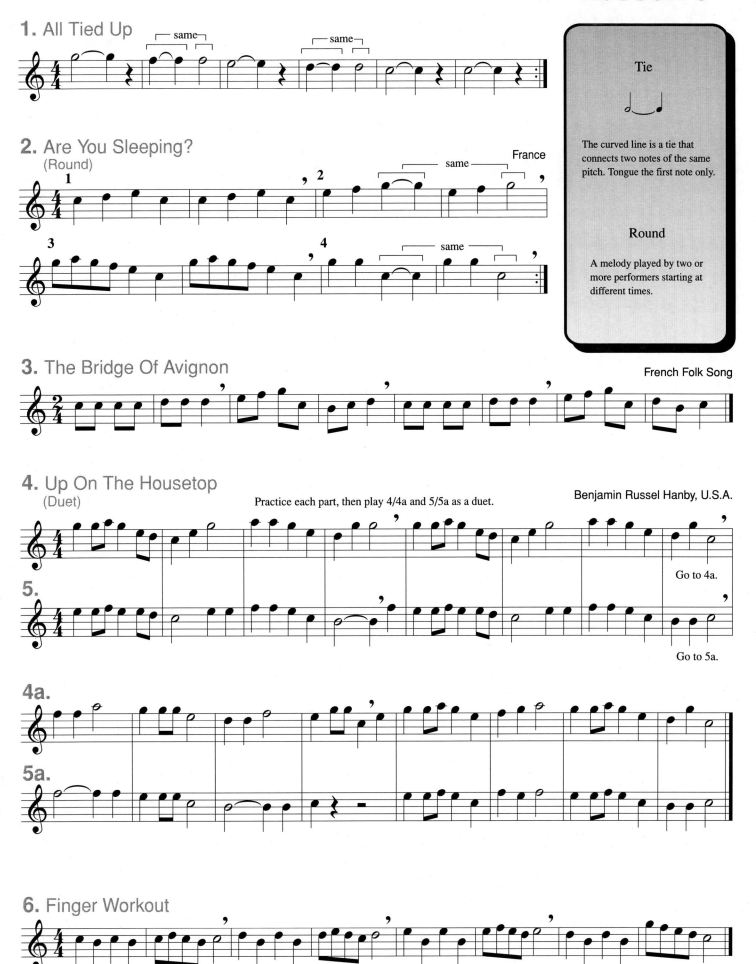

Lesson 7

3/4 Time Signature

3 - Three counts in each measure
4 - A quarter note receives one count

Dot

The Dot following a note is equal to one-half the value of that note.

1. Chiapanecas

Mexican Folk Song

2. A Jazzy Threesome

same

1 2 3   1 2 3

3. Beautiful Brown Eyes

American Folk Song

4. Long, Long Ago

Thomas Haynes Bayly, England

5. The Donkey
(Round)

Traditional

1   2   3

Extra Credit Exercise 5

6.

(Title)   (Title)

Your name

Compose your own melodies and then play each.

12

Lesson 8

1.

2. Yankee Doodle

American Folk Song

3. The Mocking Bird

American Folk Song

4. Barcarole

Jacques Offenbach, France

1. *Play 1st time only*

2. *Play 2nd time only*

second time

5. Down In The Valley

American Folk Song

1.

2.

6. Just Rockin' 'N' Rollin'
(Duet)

Practice each separately, then play as a duet.

7.

1st and 2nd endings

1.   2.

Play the first ending the first time and the second ending the second time.

Extra Credit Exercise 6

Lesson 9

Key Signature

The flats or sharps before the time signature which indicates the key center (Do)

Key of C (Do = C)

There are no sharps or flats in the Key of C

Pickup Note(s)

Note(s) in an incomplete measure before the first bar line.

Forward Repeat Sign:

Point of return (in place of the beginning) for repeated section

1. Check It Out

2. Russian Folk Dance

Ludwig van Beethoven, Germany

3. Blue Moon

Music by Richard Rodgers
Lyrics by Lorenz Hart, U.S.A.

Pick up note

© 1934 (Renewed 1962) EMI ROBBINS CATALOG INC.
and WARNER BROS. PUBLICATIONS U.S. INC.

4. Buenos Días Su Señoría

(Good Day, Your Highness)

Chilean Folk Song

Pick up notes

5. Polly Wolly Doodle

Traditional, U.S.A.

6. Carousel

(A Merry-Go-"Round")

7. Tenor Saxophone Workout

14

Lesson 10

1. Sound Familiar?

2. English Melody

Always look at the key signature before playing.   England

3. Foggy Dew   England

Key Signature
Key of F

All B's are lowered
to B flat (B♭)

Eighth Rests

Receives one-half count
in 4/4, 2/4 and 3/4 times

4. Keep 'Em Even

1 + 2 + 1 + 2 +

Extra Credit Exercise 7

5. Bingo   American Folk Song

6. Pickup Twister

Write the counting, clap the rhythms as you count out loud, then play.

a.   **b.**   **c.**   **d.**

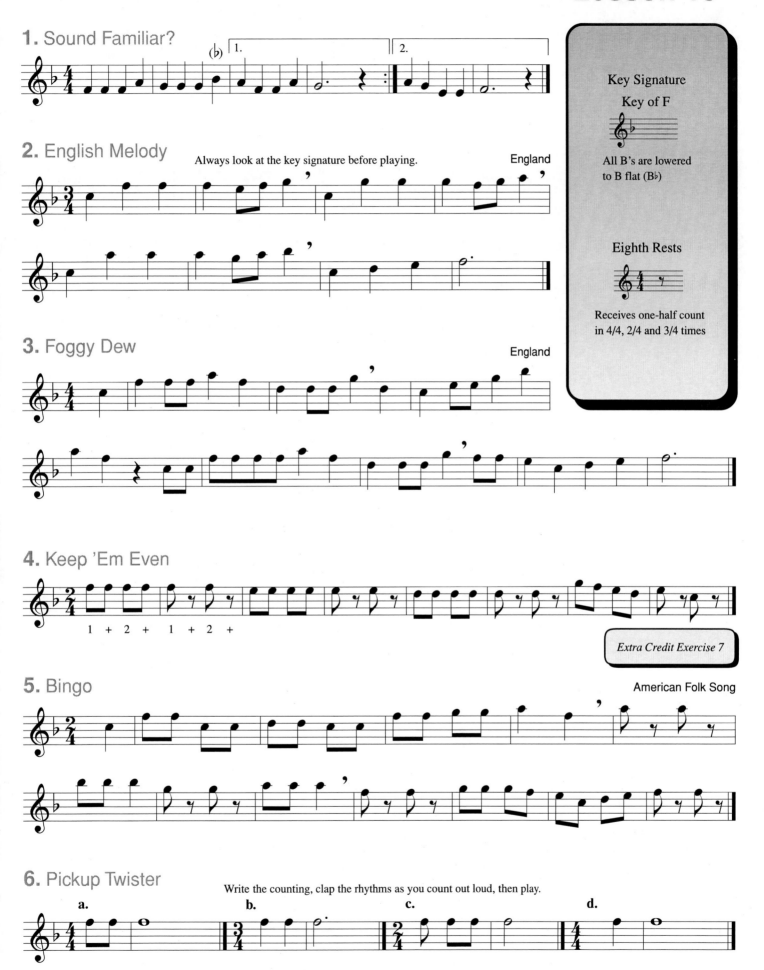

15

More Songs Just For The Fun Of It

This Old Man

American Folk Song

Tell Me Why

Traditional

Theme From Symphony № 1

Johannes Brahms, Germany

Rockin' Old Mac

Erskine MacDonald, England

This Land Is Your Land

Woody Guthrie, U.S.A.

Concert Time № 2

Theme From The Surprise Symphony

Joseph Haydn, Austria

Aura Lee

William Whiteman Fosdick
and George R. Poulton, U.S.A.

The Carnival Of Venice

Italian Folk Song

Folk Dance

Béla Bártok, Hungary

Lesson 11

Dotted quarter and eighth rhythm

1 + 2 +

Tempo

The speed of the music.
(Slow, Quick)

Ritard. - gradually slower

1.

2. Crazy Fingers

Slow   also B♭

3. Hold It!

Slow   same

Extra Credit Exercises 8 and 9

4. America

Samuel Francis Smith, U.S.A.

Quick

ritard.

5. Ecossaise

Ludwig van Beethoven, Germany

Quick

6. Tenor Saxophone Workout

1. An Accidental Encounter

2. Now Is The Month Of Maying

England

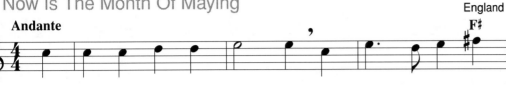

Accidentals

♯ – sharp - raises pitch one-half step
♭ – flat - lowers pitch one-half step
♮ – natural - cancels sharp or flat

Tempo

Andante - Italian word for slow
Allegro - Italian word for fast

3. The Sad Clown

Andante

4. Watch Out!

Allegro

Extra Credit Exercise 10

5. A Little Dance

Dmitri Kabalevsky, Russia

Allegro

6. Sunrise, Sunset

Lyrics by Sheldon Harnick
Music by Jerry Bock, U.S.A.

Andante

Lesson 13

1. Careful! Don't Break It!

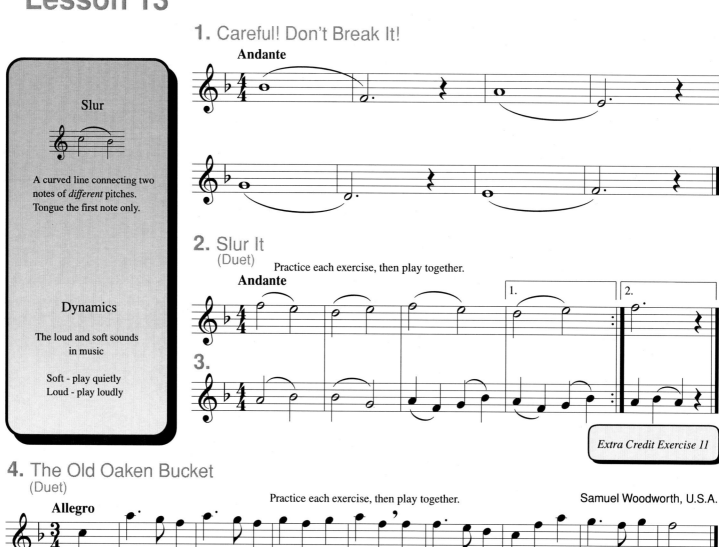

Slur

A curved line connecting two notes of *different* pitches. Tongue the first note only.

Dynamics

The loud and soft sounds in music

Soft - play quietly
Loud - play loudly

2. Slur It
(Duet)

Practice each exercise, then play together.

3.

Extra Credit Exercise 11

4. The Old Oaken Bucket
(Duet)

Practice each exercise, then play together.

Samuel Woodworth, U.S.A.

Allegro

Soft

5.

Soft

6. The Yankee Doodle Boy

George M. Cohan, U.S.A.

Allegro

Loud

Lesson 14

1. A Warmup Exercise

Andante

2. Slip, Slide and Slur

Moderato

slurs can be above or below notes

Extra Credit Exercise 12

> **Warm-up exercises**
>
> Play at the beginning of a practice session.
>
> p = Piano *(soft)*
>
> f = Forte *(loud)*
>
> **Moderato**
>
> Play at a medium tempo.

3. Erie Canal
(Duet)

Samuel Woodworth, U.S.A.

Practice each exercise, then play together.

Moderato

4.

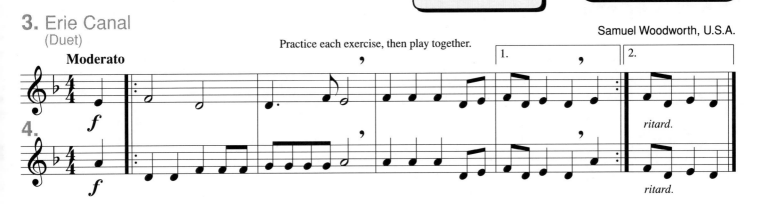

ritard.

ritard.

5. The Trolley Song

Music by Ralph Blane
Lyrics by Hugh Martin, U.S.A.

Moderato

6. Tenor Saxophone Workout

Lesson 15

Dynamics

gradually get louder   gradually get softer

mp = Moderately soft

mf = Moderately loud

rit. = *ritard.*

Afterbeats - notes which occur on the second half of the beat

1. Andante

2. On Parade
Moderato

3. Chorale
Andante

4. After Beats
Moderato

Counting: 1 + 2 + 1 + 2 + 1 + 2 + 1 + 2 1 + 2 + 1 + 2 + 1 + 2 + 1 + 2

5. More After Beats

Counting: 1 + 2 + 1 + 2 + 1 + 2 + 1 + 2 1 + 2 + 1 + 2 + 1 + 2 + 1 + 2

6. A Russian Polka
(Duet)

Extra Credit Exercise 13

Practice each exercise, then play together.

Allegro

7.

8. Rock It To Me
Allegro

22

Lesson 16

1. Etude

Moderato   Carl Czerny, Austria

Fermata

Hold the note longer than note value

Eighth and dotted quarter rhythm

2. Switcharoo

Andante

same

Extra Credit Exercise 14

3. Camptown Races

Stephen Collins Foster, U.S.A.

Moderato

rit.

4. Can You Name This Song?
(Duet)

Moderato   Practice each exercise, then play together.   Traditional

5.

Lesson 17

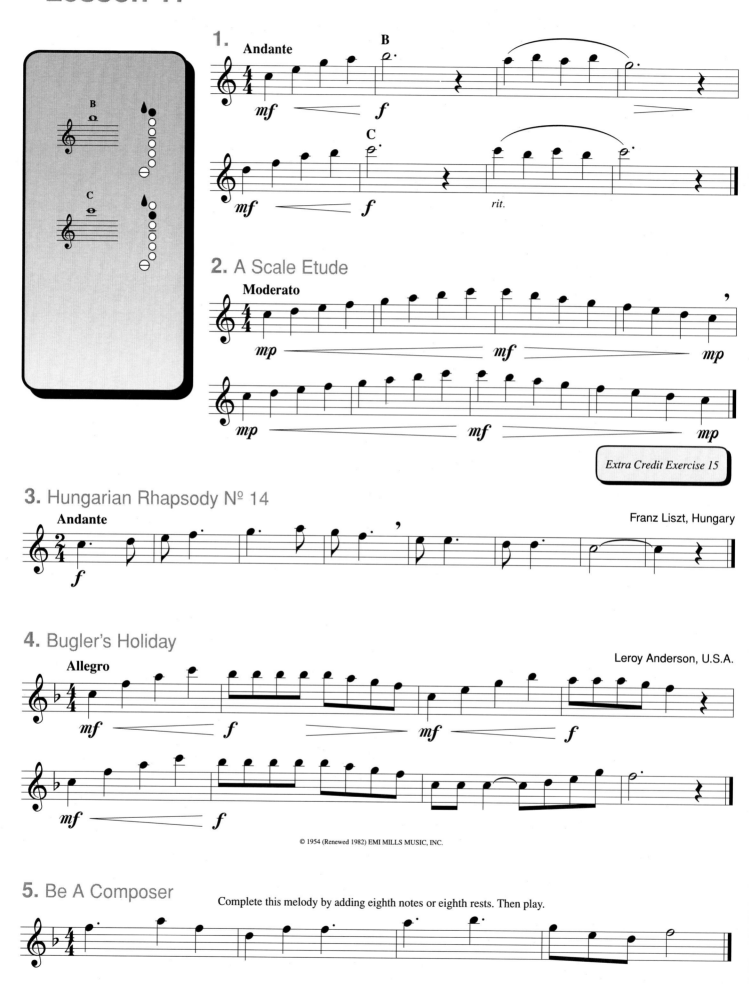

1. Andante

2. A Scale Etude

Moderato

Extra Credit Exercise 15

3. Hungarian Rhapsody № 14

Andante

Franz Liszt, Hungary

4. Bugler's Holiday

Allegro

Leroy Anderson, U.S.A.

© 1954 (Renewed 1982) EMI MILLS MUSIC, INC.

5. Be A Composer

Complete this melody by adding eighth notes or eighth rests. Then play.

Lesson 18

1. Andante

mp —— < *f*   —— *mf*

Extra Credit Exercise 16

2. Andante

mf —— < *f*   *mf* —— < *f*

mf —— > *mp*

Multiple measures rest

2 = | — — — |

Rest the amount of measures shown by the number.

3. Siranda
(Duet)

Moderato

Practice each exercise, then play together.

Portuguese Folk Song

mf

rit.

4.

mf

rit.

5. Hop, Hop, Hop
(Duet)

Allegro

Practice 5 and 6, then play together.

German Folk Song

f

2

6.

f

Count: 1   2   2   2

2

Count: 1   2   2   2

mf —— < *f*

mf —— < *f*

Still More Fun Songs

Amazing Grace

Andante

Traditional

Marine's Hymn

Allegro

Traditional, U.S.A.

Danny Boy

Andante

Frederick E. Weatherly, England

The Sidewalks Of New York

(East Side, West Side)

Charles B. Lawlor
and James W. Blake, U.S.A.

La Bamba

Mexico

CHORALE AND VARIANTS

ROBERT WASHBURN ASCAP

COMMENCEMENT
(An Overture for Band)

ROBERT W. SMITH

Extra Credit Exercises

1. *Use after lesson 1, line 8*

2. *Use after lesson 3, line 5*

3. *Use after lesson 4, line 8*

4. *Use after lesson 5, line 6*

5. *Use after lesson 7, line 5*

6. *Use after lesson 8, line 7*

7. *Use after lesson 10, line 4*

8. *Use after lesson 11, line 3*

Quick

Clap the rhythm while counting out loud, then play the exercise.

9. *Use after lesson 11, line 3*

Quick

Clap the rhythm while counting out loud, then play the exercise.

10. *Use after lesson 12, line 4*

Allegro

11. *Use after lesson 13, line 3*

Andante

12. *Use after lesson 14, line 2*

Andante

13. *Use after lesson 15, line 5*

Moderato

Clap the rhythm while counting out loud, then play the exercise.

mf

14. *Use after lesson 16, line 2*

Moderato

Clap the rhythm while counting out loud, then play the exercise.

mf

15. *Use after lesson 17, line 2*

Allegro

mp ——— *f* ——— *mp*

16. *Use after lesson 18, line 1*

Moderato

mp ——— *mf* ——— *mp*

PARTS OF A TENOR SAXOPHONE

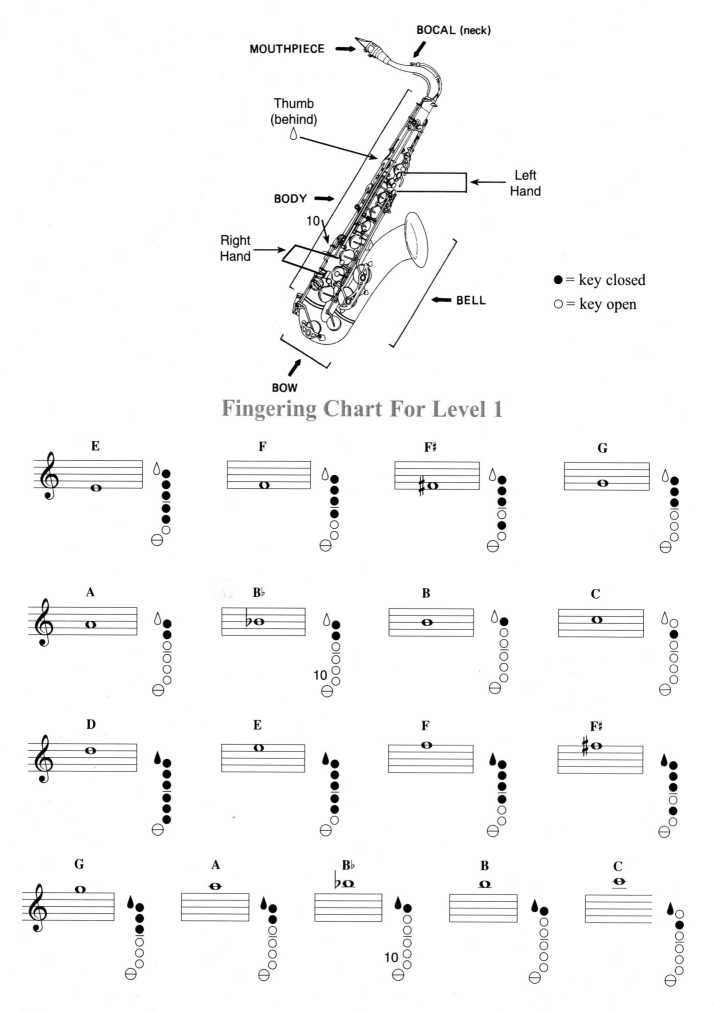

Fingering Chart For Level 1